S0-ADZ-897

The Promise and Perils of Technology™

FILTER BUBBLES
AND YOU

Carol Hand

Rosen
YA
New York

BOISE PUBLIC LIBRARY

3 1150 01717 0347

Published in 2020 by The Rosen Publishing Group, Inc.
29 East 21st Street, New York, NY 10010

Copyright © 2020 by The Rosen Publishing Group, Inc.

First Edition

All rights reserved. No part of this book may be reproduced in any form
without permission in writing from the publisher, except by a reviewer.

Library of Congress Cataloging-in-Publication Data

Names: Hand, Carol, 1945– author.
Title: Filter bubbles and you / Carol Hand.
Description: First edition. | New York: Rosen Publishing, 2020. | Series: The promise
and perils of technology | Includes bibliographical references and index.
Identifiers: LCCN 2018044834| ISBN 9781508188254
(library bound) | ISBN 9781508188247 (pbk.)
Subjects: LCSH: Electronic information resource literacy—Juvenile literature. | Web
search engines—Social aspects—Juvenile literature. | Social media—Psychological
aspects—Juvenile literature. | Filter bubbles (Information filtering)—Juvenile literature.
| Internet—Moral and ethical aspects—Juvenile literature. | Mass media—Objectivity.
Classification: LCC ZA3085 .H35 2020 | DDC 025.5/24—dc23
LC record available at https://lccn.loc.gov/2018044834

Manufactured in the United States of America

CONTENTS

INTRODUCTION

On November 8, 2016, the United States was rocked by the election of Donald Trump. It was an event almost no one expected. People who disliked Donald Trump and assumed Hillary Clinton would win were asking, "How could this happen?" Even Trump supporters, ecstatic at his win, were surprised.

Some people, including Drake Baer writing for The Cut, think people were blindsided by Trump's election because Americans today live in filter bubbles. That is, most people take in only information with which they agree. They are seldom, if ever, exposed to opposing views. According to Baer, this filtering occurs because many people get their news from social media, which is personalized to give them the news they want. In 2016, Facebook reached 67 percent of US adults, with 40 percent of them obtaining news. Google, in 2016, used more than two hundred signals taken from each user's search history to determine what news stories the user would prefer to see. According to Baer, most people live in a bubble designed by filtering their online content to fit their personal interests and beliefs. He thinks these filter bubbles explain why so many people were totally unaware of the electorate's turn toward Trump.

Carleigh Morgan, writing for Motherboard, disagrees. According to Morgan, filter bubbles on social media such as Facebook are a symptom, rather than of a cause, of Trump's election or other surprising events. Morgan points out that filter bubbles are not static, but interactive. They become more precise and nuanced as they receive more information from the user's online activity. That is, interactions of users with a social media platform form a feedback loop in which users participate in creating their own filter bubbles. Morgan notes that people talk of "bursting" filter bubbles to free themselves from the restrictions of their online persona. However, she points out that digital

Many people today get most, or all, of their news from online sources. Here, a man reads the online version of the *New York Times* on his iPad.

platforms are not necessarily restrictive. Bursting the bubble will not suddenly free the user—because social media is not the only filter bubble in which people exist. Although the term was coined for social media, people's entire lives are often lived in filter bubbles.

People who live in a neighborhood where everyone drives a new BMW or Lexus have a different worldview from those living in a neighborhood where many drive older cars if they own cars at all. People associate with family members, friends, and workmates who expose them to a certain set of beliefs. They go to churches and schools, belong to clubs or organizations, read books and magazines or watch television news, all of which steer them toward a particular viewpoint. Whether he or she realizes it or not, every person has a worldview, or lives in a filter bubble, shaped by his or her life experiences. Social media is not the only platform that does this filtering. It is simply the newest—and perhaps the most efficient—platform for the filter bubble.

Making Sense of Filter Bubbles

I n December 2009, the search engine Google introduced a change that made only a small splash at the time. The announcement that Google would begin personalizing everyone's search results attracted only about fifty total news articles and blog posts, according to Danny Sullivan, writing for Search Engine Land. But that change, Sullivan noted in his article, was "the biggest change that has ever happened in search engines." Previously, everyone who typed in the same search words received the same set of results—or almost the same set. Results varied somewhat based on country—US and UK searchers, for example, received slightly different lists. But now, every individual doing a Google search would receive a search list tailored to his or her own needs and interests.

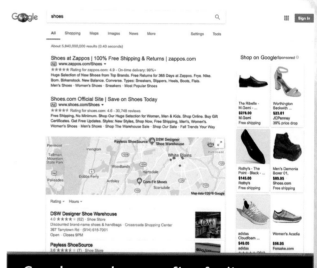

Google searches are often for items such as shoes. Google uses all searches, including those for items, political content, and information, to develop personalized searches for each individual.

What Is a Filter Bubble?

A filter bubble is the cocoon of information, typically online content, with which internet users typically surround themselves. It is the set of information they receive through Facebook, Twitter, Google, and other online sources. No one sees all the information available on a given subject. Each person sees only a small percentage of the deluge

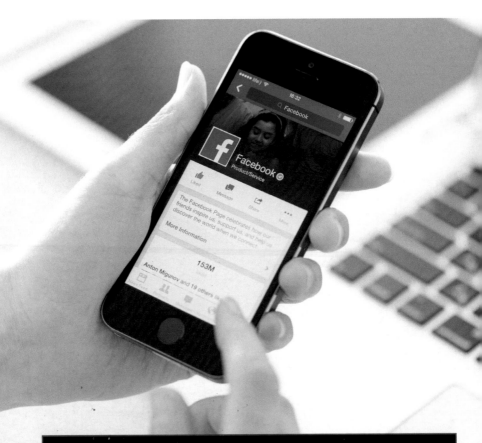

Past searches show what each person prefers to view, and Facebook uses this information to develop a user profile. This user views her profile on an iPhone.

of available information. What the person sees first is what he or she will most likely prefer. The selection, or filtering, is done not by the individual, but by the online provider, for example, Facebook. Facebook determines a person's preferences partly by keeping track of what the person has clicked on in the past. It also collects information on the kind of computer the person is using, his or her browser, and his or her location. With enough information, Facebook or Google can accurately determine the kind of information a person prefers. The viewer never sees what has been edited out. Everyone receives information that is biased, or at least incomplete. The result is that everyone, often without realizing it, lives in his or her own filter bubble.

The online encyclopedia Techopedia defines a filter bubble as the intellectual isolation that results when websites make assumptions

Judging a Website

There are several ways to avoid filter bubbles and conduct an unbiased search. First, regularly clear the search engine's browsing history. Second, search incognito. Some search engines, such as DuckDuckGo and StartPage, do not collect search histories. Other browsers have "incognito" or "private" modes that a researcher can turn on before searching. Third, begin by getting background information on a topic, including opposing viewpoints. Then, search using keywords to avoid missing important information. Fourth, learn to recognize and use only trustworthy websites. Double-check sources, and trace information and quotations back to their original source. This step helps ensure the accuracy of the information. Finally, use library databases. These databases use only high-quality sources and do not filter searches.

about what users want to see and selectively give them only that information. In Google, this situation results in people searching for the same keywords but receiving different lists of websites. One example was given by Eli Pariser in the introduction to his 2011 book, *The Filter Bubble*. In spring 2010, during the British Petroleum (BP) Deepwater Horizon oil spill, he asked two fairly similar friends to search for the keyword "BP." One received mostly news about the oil spill. The other received investment information for BP, but nothing about the oil spill. Regardless of what they search for, people in filter bubbles become intellectually isolated because they have little or no contact with information that contradicts, or lies outside, their own interests and beliefs.

Eli Pariser Warns About Filter Bubbles

The term "filter bubble" was coined by Eli Pariser in his 2011 book of the same name. Pariser is best known as a liberal activist who uses the power of social media to initiate social and political change. He was the executive director of the progressive organization MoveOn from 2004 until 2008. In 2012, he cofounded Upworthy, a site that collects and packages uplifting stories into short, entertaining clips.

When Pariser was growing up in the 1990s, he believed the World Wide Web would be great for democracy because it would connect everyone in the world. He visualized all information being available to everyone. But as Google, Facebook, and other companies began to filter web content, his vision became less likely. Pariser describes in his 2011 TED talk how he first became aware of the effects of filtering. Although Pariser leans left politically, he also followed conservative, or right-leaning, friends on Facebook. He wanted to see what conservatives were thinking, to learn from them, even sometimes argue with them. Then, suddenly, he noticed that all of his conservative friends disappeared from his Facebook feed.

Eli Pariser, author of the 2011 book *The Filter Bubble*, speaks at a conference in Austin, Texas, on the topic "Do Algorithms Dream of Viral Content?"

Facebook, without consulting him, had decided that he preferred liberal sites, and simply deleted all conservative sites. With research, Pariser figured out that, because he clicked more often on liberal sites than on conservative ones, Facebook had responded by giving him the content it thought he wanted to see. He emphasizes that Facebook made the decision without his input. It had put him in a filter bubble where he saw only liberal-leaning information.

When the news industry was mostly controlled by newspapers, radio, and television, the gatekeepers who decided what readers

Four Types of Filter Bubbles

Filtering algorithms can be roughly divided into four types, according to a framework proposed by French sociologist Dominique Cardon and described by Pierre-Nicolas Schwab, writing for IntoTheMinds. These types are based on four kinds of web measurements— views, links, likes, and traces. The key difference among types is the gatekeeper.

The first type is based on views, or audience measurements; that is, how many clicks or views a site receives. The gatekeeper algorithm makes decisions independent of the content, and the audience has the power to switch.

The second type is based on the user's decision to click on links in the original file. If a user clicks on a link, the file's ranking increases. In a search engine such as Google, Google's rules are not known to the user; the user gives up authority.

The third type results when "social gatekeepers" or influencers comment on a site. For example, people who retweet in Twitter or click "Like" on Facebook determine the popularity of the tweet or site. Most power is concentrated in a few hands; for example, famous people are much more influential than unknown people.

In the fourth type, users are their own gatekeepers. For example, Netflix traces a person's previous watching history and uses it to recommend new movies or television shows. Often, people follow these recommendations, which limits the media they consume. People can consciously choose to change, but they usually don't.

or viewers saw were human editors. Those gatekeepers were (and are) not perfect and they have biases, but they do follow a code of conduct with a built-in ethical component. Most try to give their consumers a relatively balanced range of news, and they practice social responsibility—that is, they do not push hate, violence, or rumors that are not reliably sourced. Pariser fears that, as computer programs rather than people become the only gatekeepers, the news individuals see is much less likely to be important, uncomfortable, or thought provoking. People will see only what is in their filter bubble. They will not be challenged and they will not learn. Pariser likens this situation to consuming a diet of junk food or eating only desserts, rather than eating a balanced diet.

From Balanced News to Filter Bubbles

At a newspaper, the human editors analyze incoming news stories and decide which ones the paper will cover. They choose major stories in all areas, including politics, national events, local events, sports, and entertainment. Most of the same stories are covered in all papers, although different editors and writers might emphasize different aspects of a story. But professional journalists follow the SPJ Code of Ethics, a statement by the Society of Professional Journalists that outlines the principles of fair and accurate journalism.

Social media has digital, not human, gatekeepers. Social media platforms use algorithms to filter incoming information and either accept or reject it. An algorithm is a set of rules, or a process used for problem solving. Filtering algorithms incorporate vast amounts of personal information collected about individual computer users and use it to decide what the user sees. These algorithms do not judge information based on truth, accuracy, or even content. The user receives a hodgepodge of information. Some of it is misleading

Killed by runaway truck

In newsrooms, human editors serve as gatekeepers of information. Here, editor Andrew Harrod previews the front page of the *Barnsley Chronicle*, in Barnsley, England.

or incorrect, and some is strongly biased toward particular social or political views.

Although Eli Pariser defined filter bubbles in 2011, the public largely overlooked them until the 2016 presidential election. Many people saw the combined influence of filter bubbles and fake news (rumors or propaganda spread intentionally through the media) as key factors in Trump's win. In 2017, some social media business owners, such as Mark Zuckerberg of Facebook, responded with changes designed to improve the platform's level of social responsibility.

How Filter Bubbles Work

Filter bubbles change people's lives by limiting the information they see. People encounter filter bubbles across all social media platforms—Facebook, Google, Snapchat, Twitter, Amazon, and others. But how are filter bubbles made? First, they require a large number of people to sign on to the same media platform. Some people sign on to communicate with friends. Others want to obtain news or information or buy something. Whatever the reason, every time a person signs on, the platform collects more personal information about that person. Statisticians create algorithms that filter the information, defining what each person likes most. These algorithms enable the platform to give the user a personalized experience. They also flood the individual's page with advertisements they will likely respond to.

Collecting Personal Information

To join Facebook, users must provide their name, gender, birthdate, and email or telephone number. Facebook also encourages users to add other personal information, such as location, photos, education and work history, family and relationships, among other items. Facebook stores it all. In addition, Facebook keeps track of everything users do when logged in. This activity includes all IP addresses used to log in, a complete list of friends (including deleted friends), every

```
<interceptors>
  <interceptor-stack name="defaultWithoutUpload"
    <interceptor-ref name="exception"/>
    <interceptor-ref name="alias"/>
    <interceptor-ref name="servletConfig"/>
    <interceptor-ref name="i18n"/>
    <interceptor-ref name="prepare"/>
    <interceptor-ref name="chain"/>
    <interceptor-ref name="scopedModelDriven"/
    <interceptor-ref name="modelDriven"/>
    <interceptor-ref name="checkbox"/>
    <interceptor-ref name="datetime"/>
```

For every algorithm, programmers create computer code to make applications work. Sometimes code filters information to create personalized searches; sometimes it runs applications such as Java, as seen here.

post, every "like," every status change, every time the user is tagged in another's post, every ad clicked on, and every search.

Facebook also stores information on third-party apps—those that allow Facebook users to log in using their Facebook password. These include apps such as Candy Crush, Airbnb, Spotify, and Uber. The third-party apps also collect various types of information, and they are free to sell it to other organizations, such as the behavioral analysis firm Strategic Communications Laboratories. Data from Facebook and third-party apps is also sold on the dark web. This part of the web requires special software to log in and caters to markets involving drugs, terrorism, weapons sales, and other illegal activities.

Gatekeeping Theory

Gatekeeping did not begin with social media. Psychologist Kurt Lewin first used the term in 1947 to describe any person who decides what passes through each gate, or decision-making step, of any process. For example, he identified the wife or mother as the gatekeeper who determines what food the family eats. In the 1950s, journalism professor David M. White applied gatekeeping to journalism. In the 1970s, Maxwell McCombs and Donald Shaw described how the gatekeeper's decisions affect an audience. They pointed out that the importance an audience attaches to news items is based on how much gatekeepers, or editors, emphasize them. Gatekeepers filter the information; they decide which stories the public sees and which they do not. Or, within a story, they decide which details to emphasize, de-emphasize, or omit. In political or social situations, this determination creates a specific picture of world events—a picture designed by the gatekeeper's control of the flow of information. This ability to shape political or social reality is known as agenda setting. For example, the Fox News organization generally sets an agenda strongly biased toward right-wing politics. Gatekeeping and agenda-setting today also occur in social media outlets, through filter bubbles.

Google has similar masses of information on every user. They collect location information, so they have a record of every place a person has been since the first day they began using Google on their phone. They store a complete search history, even deleted searches. Their advertisement profile on each user, based on search history, determines what ads the user sees. Google knows every app a person uses, how often he or she uses it, where he or she uses it, and with

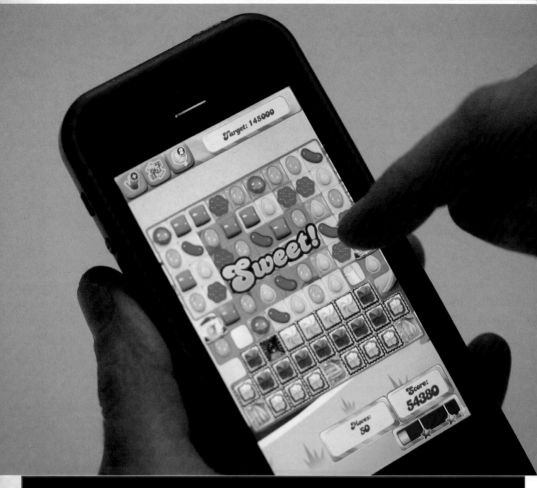

This Candy Crush Saga player likely logged in via Facebook. The Candy Crush app has collected all of the user's Facebook information and may sell it to other organizations.

whom he or she interacts. They have the user's complete YouTube history. They have every email ever sent or received, including those deleted or marked as spam.

When analyzed by algorithms, this user information leads to personalized search results in Google and personalized news feeds in Facebook. In both cases, it results in personalized ad targeting.

How Algorithms Work

Google almost instantly searches billions of webpages to answer search questions. It monitors and measures hundreds of characteristics making up each website. A few of these include URLs, content, internal links, external links, images, and speed. One group of algorithms analyzes the meaning of search words. One group judges and filters content; another group judges links. Some algorithms organize. Some collect data into a format that users can understand. Google's search algorithms rank sources primarily on the basis of two characteristics: authoritativeness, or how often other sites link to the site, and relevance, or how well the site's content fits the question. For the question, "Are reptiles bad pets?" a site containing the words "reptiles," "bad," and "pets" ranks higher than one with the words "reptiles," "good," and "pets."

At one time, Google had a relatively simple algorithm, but as the number and complexity of websites increased, the complexity of the algorithm increased, too. Today, Google consists of many small, independent algorithms, each with its own function. Each algorithm interacts and shares information with the others. This structure enables the search engine to consider additional factors without accidentally damaging other parts of the system. Many small algorithms form a whole algorithm that is much greater than the sum of its parts.

The same is true for other social media outlets. In January 2018, Google admitted to having a filter-bubble problem; that is, its searches reinforce the searcher's bias. Google plans to solve this problem by training its search engine to understand the intent of searchers' questions. For example, a filter-bubble search provides different results to searches for "Are reptiles good pets?" versus "Are reptiles bad pets?" A revised search would interpret the question as "How do reptiles rate as pets?" and would provide information on both sides of the question. Google plans to introduce its updates in stages. Solutions for complex, biased, or controversial searches, such as those on politics or climate change, will be introduced last because it is more difficult to modify the search engine for these.

Filter Bubbles and Echo Chambers

People tend to seek out information sources that strengthen their pre-existing beliefs and assumptions. People use this confirmation bias in their everyday lives, in and out of social media. Teens surround themselves with a clique of friends who shower them with praise and never criticize. A politically conservative person may choose to watch only Fox News. Social media algorithms pick up on these pre-existing biases and design a filter bubble that ensures that the person receives only that biased information. On Facebook or Snapchat, teens interact only with their friends. Fox News viewers receive only right-wing viewpoints. Within these filter bubbles, the user's existing confirmation bias is strengthened. This situation, in which people's ideas and beliefs are reinforced because they hear them over and over, is also sometimes called an echo chamber or opinion cluster. Information is exchanged within an echo chamber, but very little is exchanged between two opposing echo chambers.

According to Nick Lum, writing for Medium, the terms "echo chamber" and "filter bubble" have different uses. The term "echo chamber" is usually meant to be insulting. For example, "He surrounds himself with people who don't contradict him; he lives in his own echo chamber." The term "filter bubble" is most often used by people to refer to their own situation. It is neutral and does not imply blame or carry insulting connotations. Alice Thwaite, writing for EchoChamber.club, states that academics use the term

Teens collaborate on class projects and share news and information via social media. If they share only with their friends, they may exist within a filter bubble of similar information.

"filter bubble" to refer only to online methods of personalization or polarization—those carried out by algorithms for Google, Facebook, and the like. Echo chambers also include outside information sources. Thwaite describes them in her article as "algorithms plus pub culture." They include interactions with friends and colleagues and information gained from offline media, such as television, magazines, and newspapers. This description suggests that echo chambers have been around as long as human communities. Filter bubbles are new.

The Fake News Connection

Often, a person's reality is controlled by the filter bubble or echo chamber in which he or she lives. What if the information in that filter bubble or echo chamber is false? What if it is run by someone with a damaging or even criminal agenda? How would the user know?

The Russian government interfered in the 2016 US elections using fake Facebook and Instagram ads. Many members of Congress criticized social media companies for allowing these ads to run.

Would he or she even care if it fit his or her biased worldview? The rise of fake news adds this alarming aspect to the idea of filter bubbles and echo chambers. Fake news is news that is false, but deliberately packaged to appear true. Its intent is to deceive the consumer.

Some critics of social media place the blame for election upsets, such as the election of Donald Trump, on the rapid spread of fake news through social media. For example, two 2016 studies showed the importance of botnets in spreading fake news during the 2016 presidential campaign. Botnets are internet-connected computers that communicate with each other and coordinate their actions. They are often used to send spam. After the election, multiple news outlets, including the *Washington Post*, Daily Beast, and *Independent* (United Kingdom), reported that thousands of Russian botnets had spread massive amounts of fake news targeting Hillary Clinton and favoring Donald Trump. In May 2018, the Daily Beast reported that the Federal Bureau of Investigation (FBI) had seized control of a key server controlling Russia's botnets, in an attempt to prevent future election interference.

In both filter bubbles and echo chambers, data gathering is biased and personalized, the free exchange of ideas is limited, and people seldom or never hear competing or contradictory ideas. New or different ideas may exist on the outside, but people inside an echo chamber or filter bubble never hear them. Fake news makes this situation worse.

The Pros and Cons of Filter Bubbles

The concept of personalized social media started out as a good thing. People appreciate the personal touch—the barista who remembers your name and order, the teacher who writes an encouraging note on your term paper, the friend who remembers your birthday with a special gift. Personalization algorithms extended this feel-good approach to social media. Consumers felt valued. They were more likely to respond positively to ads, benefiting both the media platform and the advertisers. Social media personalization occurred rapidly. Only later did people begin to consider its negative as well as its positive effects.

The Benefits of Filter Bubbles

Aline Oliveira, on the Digital Marketing Blog at the University of Brighton in England, explains that personalization began for very practical reasons. Suppose a user wants to know about Taylor Swift's latest recording. A search for her name returns 410,000,000 hits. Nobody can search a list that long, so the search engine makes an educated guess, based on the user's past activity. It assumes the person wants either Swift's latest recording or her tour schedule. It puts both on the first page of the search list, where they are instantly viewable. Personalization makes finding the desired information faster and more efficient. As a search engine learns more about an individual, it can give individuals more of what they want. It can pinpoint their favorite music, books, and films; the types of things they like to see, from puppy videos to lists of haunted houses; and the types of things they will likely buy.

Online users are happier when they receive personalized content and experiences they relate to. Websites and apps are supported by advertising, and marketers are happier because they know what users want and can sell more by targeting them personally. Users see many examples of personalized filters but may not recognize them. According to Oliveira, the Amazon recommendations feature that says "Customers who bought this item also bought" is responsible for 35 percent of Amazon's sales. Netflix lets consumers rank titles and then recommends other content the user would be interested in. Tumblr tracks tags that people use most often and recommends new tags that might interest them. Facebook's "Top Stories" news

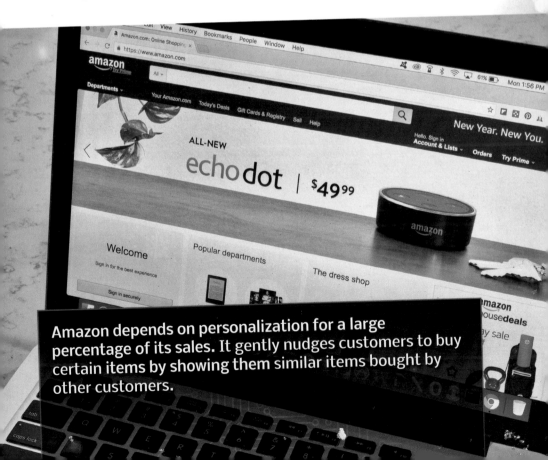

Amazon depends on personalization for a large percentage of its sales. It gently nudges customers to buy certain items by showing them similar items bought by other customers.

feed, Twitter's "Top Tweets" setting, and iTunes "Top Apps" and "Top Songs" are all examples of personalization.

Another benefit of social media personalization is the ability to connect with others having similar interests. Online networking

Teens and Filter Bubbles

Does teens' use of social media translate into being inside a filter bubble? Yes and no. According to a 2018 Pew Research Center study, about 95 percent of US teens ages thirteen to seventeen have a smartphone and 45 percent say they are almost constantly online. The top five sites they use are YouTube, Instagram, Snapchat, Facebook, and Twitter. Snapchat is most popular; YouTube is second. Teens use social media primarily for interacting with friends and family, so in that sense, they live in a filter bubble of like-minded people. Teens also use social media to meet others with similar interests. Some obtain news from social media. This situation suggests that they are receiving news with which they agree, but the study did not address this point.

According to Christine Elgersma on Common Sense Media, some sites, including Snapchat and Whisper, are considered self-destructing or secret. That is, a photo or video will disappear after a set time limit. However, people can take a screenshot while the photo is online, or it can be recovered later. Some apps are public, so teens may chat or share videos or photos with strangers. Instagram's default setting is public. Many teens post items to increase their popularity; thus, many strangers see their posts. Retweeting on Twitter and reblogging on Tumblr can spread teens' posts far and wide. The results may either broaden the teens' world or become dangerous. In either case, they have left their filter bubbles.

can open up opportunities for learning and career advancement. Jeffrey Weldon, writing on a blog for Georgetown University design students, gives the example of a student interested in creative writing who connected with an online creative writing community. This connection gave her an opportunity to share her interest and to learn. She was also offered a summer job in creative writing. Such opportunities are available to people of all interests, from coding to science to video making to art and music.

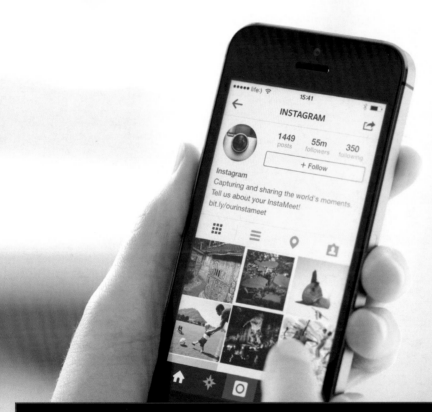

Instagram is an important medium for connecting with friends and the wider world. Such connections can provide opportunities to explore hobbies, careers, and life opportunities.

The Drawbacks of Filter Bubbles

Eli Pariser outlined his concerns about filter bubbles in 2011, and many people share these concerns. The major unintended consequence of personalization is isolation. This outcome may not be too serious if the user is trapped in a filter bubble surrounded by his or her favorite music and movies. But users who are too isolated politically or socially may risk knowing nothing about important world events or having no exposure to controversial, but vitally important, ideas. Oliveira points out that people getting their news from a newspaper can skip the front page and go straight to the sports section. But at least they see the front-page headlines and know if something catastrophic is happening. However, a person who lives in an online sports-only filter bubble might totally miss the fact that—for example—the country has just declared war.

Filtering simplifies people's lives—not just how they conduct their lives, but what they learn, understand, and think about. An important aspect of creativity is making connections across different subject areas. A scientist working on artificial intelligence might benefit by considering biological information, such as what makes humans or other kinds of animals intelligent. Missing this connection might prevent a breakthrough. Lee Carnihan, writing for LinkedIn, notes that, although some filtering is a good thing, too much is not. People fail to learn things they want and need to know. They might not receive information outside their filter bubble that could enrich their lives and careers. Carnihan suggests one solution for too much filtering: open-minded filtering. He proposes that content filters could occasionally let in "awesome and random content," even when it is outside an individual's filter bubble. If something is unusual enough, the person might be interested in it. Even occasional information from outside the filter bubble would broaden and enrich a person's life.

Apple News versus Facebook News

In January 2018, Facebook stated that it planned to improve its News Feed feature by making it "more fulfilling" and "good for your well-being," according to Callum Borchers in the *Washington Post*. The Facebook plan included placing even more emphasis on information liked, posted, and shared by members of the user's own social networks. They would place less emphasis on corporate brands and on posts from outside the users' networks. In practice, Borchers says, this action means the user will receive a constant barrage of information with which they agree. Their filter bubble will grow even stronger.

Apple is taking a contrasting approach. In June 2018, they announced a new section on their Apple News app highlighting news on the 2018 midterm elections. Karissa Bell, writing for Mashable, states that the new section, like the entire app, is managed by human editors, not algorithms. These human gatekeepers choose fact-based stories from highly reputable sources and many different publishers. Bell describes the new section as an antidote to the filter bubbles generated by Facebook's feel-good approach. According to editor-in-chief Lauren Kern of Apple News, as reported by Bell, the new feature will not avoid controversy, but the goal is "to illuminate, not enrage." They plan to avoid rumor and propaganda. But in a section called "the conversation," they will feature opinion columns emphasizing all sides of an issue and originating from a variety of news sources.

Bill Gates is concerned that filter bubbles are isolating people. Here, Gates speaks at the Goalkeepers 2017 conference, sponsored by the Bill & Melinda Gates Foundation, in New York City.

Bill Gates, cofounder of Microsoft, is also concerned about filter bubbles. In an article by Kevin J. Delaney in Quartz, Gates says he fears filter bubbles are a danger to good citizenship because if citizens have such polarized sources of information, they have no common basis for connection or agreement. Also, the algorithms used by Facebook and others operate in the background, so users have no idea what is being filtered out—or even that filtering is occurring. Many people actually seek out sites that give them little information, or incorrect information, Gates says. This situation results in people having extremely narrow worldviews. Gates thinks filter bubbles may ultimately be self-correcting because bad information leads to bad outcomes. He cites as an example people whose filter bubble constantly tells them not to use vaccines. Gates sees education, which provides a common base of knowledge, as the best way to counteract the isolation imposed by filter bubbles.

Filter bubbles have both advantages and disadvantages. Having a general, broad-based education, as Bill Gates recommends, will help counteract their disadvantages. Social media users can also learn how algorithms work to form filter bubbles and how they can "burst" their own filter bubbles. This knowledge would give consumers more control over their use of social media.

The Ethics of Filter Bubbles

Every time a new technology develops, new moral and ethical issues arise. Social media is no exception. Ethical questions related to social media indicate where ethical principles need to be defined and enforced in this new field. These include the collection and use of personal information, the rise of cyberbullying, and the use of social media to influence elections.

Former New York Assembly Speaker Sheldon Silver leaves federal court in July 2018 after being sentenced to prison for bribery and money laundering. Ethical violations are common in politics.

Defining Ethics

Ethics deals with questions of right and wrong. It affects how people live and make decisions and helps them define their rights and responsibilities. It leads individuals to consider how their actions affect other individuals and society. Ethical rules help people understand how to live a good life. They are meant to strengthen society. However, if one segment of society considers something to be wrong, these individuals may use their ethical stance as a weapon against those who disagree. This

Ethical or Not? A Checklist

Making an ethical decision is challenging. Many decisions result in both good and bad outcomes. Dr. Laura Hills, on the website Blue Pencil Sharpener, suggests a series of questions people can ask if they are conflicted about the ethics of an action.

- What are the outcomes of the action?
- Who will benefit? How and how much?
- Who will suffer? How and how much?
- Why do I personally want to do this action?
- Why do I want my business or employer to do this?
- Is it legal, or does it have legal consequences?
- How would I feel if this were on the front page or the television news?
- Will I respect myself more or less if I do this?
- Will others respect me more or less if I do this?
- Does it feel right, or does it give me unpleasant physical symptoms?
- Would I want this done to me? Does this action damage or help our business?
- Would my mentor, hero, or any highly ethical person approve of this action?

situation is evident in social polarization over issues such as abortion and gun rights.

The words "ethics" and "morals" are often used interchangeably. Morals tend to be more subjective and based on personal or religious attitudes. Ethics are practical and focus on interactions in business and society. A politician involved in a sex scandal is violating a subjective moral law. A politician taking a bribe from a company he is charged with regulating is violating a practical code of ethics. But these situations do overlap; each has both moral and ethical components. Because most examples in life have both components, people seldom distinguish clearly between the two concepts.

Collection of Personal Information

People get what they want, but not necessarily what they need, from a personalized online search. They might not get what is arguably the most important information. Personalized searches are convenient and relevant, and they please people. But are they ethical? No, according to Hannah Smith, writing for Moz.com. Smith says, "We are handing over control to an algorithm that **by design** does not strive to provide a balanced mix of results."

The results are not balanced because nothing in the algorithm is based on criteria used by responsible journalists or researchers. The algorithm bases its search on relevance to the individual, by looking at that person's previous searches. It does not choose thoughtful or even rational content. When people share on social media, they most often share highly emotional, especially negative, content. Filters return search content that is also emotional, impulsive, and negative. This content then reinforces that bias—a filter bubble—that increases polarization. Konrad Lischka and Christian Stöcker, writing for The Conversation, recommend that algorithm developers change their methods to improve this process. They suggest opening the process to outside researchers, sharing algorithms with consumers, making algorithms more diverse, and establishing a code of ethics for developers.

Cloud computing has led to an immense amount of user data, combined with massive amounts of computer power and storage. Personalization algorithms are needed to help the user process

Cloud computing enables storage of massive amounts of data on remote servers. Algorithms can sort through and personalize this "big data," but the algorithms remove control from the user.

this information overload. But algorithms are not values neutral. Information technologists Engin Bozdag and Job Timmermans suggest three ways to improve algorithms by giving the user more control. First, allow users to have different identities since information needs can vary by context. Second, allow users to customize their filters, and third, show users the criteria being used for filtering.

Cyberbullying

As the use of social media has increased, cyberbullying has risen with it. Bullying once occurred in person or over the telephone. Now people—children, teens, and adults—are bullied through social media platforms such as Facebook, Instagram, Snapchat, and Twitter or through text messaging, instant messaging, or email. Cyberbullying includes posting or sharing harmful, false, or negative content about another person. Cyberbullies spread rumors, send hurtful or threatening messages, or post unflattering or sexually suggestive photos. Some break into others' accounts to send damaging messages. They share personal information to humiliate the person. This information may never disappear completely.

Cyberbullying can spread hateful messages to a wide audience, causing shame and humiliation for the bullied person. These feelings can lead to depression, and even suicide.

Teens see social media as primarily positive. But they also recognize its negative aspects, especially cyberbullying. Cyberbullying extends the school filter bubble online, giving students a bigger audience to spread hate and belittle people. On social media, people are more willing to be hateful and mean because they can be anonymous. More than half of teens and adolescents have suffered from cyberbullying, according to the website BullyingStatistics.org. More than half also say they themselves have engaged in cyberbullying. Cyberbullying can cause teens to suffer from anxiety and depression. At worst, it has led to suicides and other violent acts.

According to a 2015 study at the University of Alberta, reported by Stephanie Pappas in *Scientific American*, there is an especially strong link between cyberbullying and depression. Depression is particularly likely in young people who both cyberbully and are bullied themselves. Serious forms of cyberbullying are increasingly prosecuted as crimes. As of 2018, nearly half of US states have added cyberbullying or electronic harassment to their laws against bullying, according to FindLaw.com.

Influencing Elections

Hacking, or stealing information by breaking into computers, spawned the new field of cybersecurity, which develops techniques to strengthen computer security. Yet, as cybersecurity improves, so do hacking and other methods of compromising online data. One ethical affront was the Russian government's attempt to influence the 2016 US presidential election through hacking and spread of online disinformation. The Russians' goal was to create discord among American voters, while supporting the Trump campaign and hurting Hillary Clinton's campaign.

Timothy Summers owns Summers & Company, an advisory firm dealing with cybersecurity issues. Summers, who calls himself an ethical hacker, notes that disinformation and social media have become the hacker's best tools. Social media enables anyone to spread

Cyberbullying in the White House

In May 2018, First Lady Melania Trump launched her Be Best campaign, focusing on child-related issues, including positive behavior on social media. In August 2018, she spoke at a cyberbullying prevention summit hosted by the Health Resources and Services Administration. Her message stressed the well-being of children and the necessity of teaching them to act safely and positively online.

Many people noted the irony of the First Lady speaking against cyberbullying while her husband, President Donald Trump, sent angry tweets insulting individuals who offended or disagreed with him. Kate Bennett and Betsy Klein of CNN reported on the president's tweets during the same week that his wife spoke against cyberbullying. He referred to former Central Intelligence Agency (CIA) director John Brennan, who had been critical of him, as a "hack" and "the worst CIA director in our country's history." He described Omarosa Manigault Newman, a former White House staffer who wrote a book critical of Trump, as a "dog" and a "crazed, crying lowlife."

The contrast between the First Lady's positive message and the president's negative tweets put the First Lady in an ethical dilemma. According to Sarah McCammon on National Public Radio (NPR), Mrs. Trump said she has told her husband she disapproves of his tweeting activity. But she said his actions will not deter her from fighting against cyberbullying.

disinformation rapidly and widely, by manipulating people rather than technology. The Russians accomplished this effort in two ways. First, they coordinated the hacking of about five hundred US people and institutions. They downloaded large amounts of potentially damaging information and released it in the weeks just before the election. The most famous example were the emails leaked from the Democratic National Committee.

Second, the Russians set up a network of troll farms, including the Internet Research Agency (IRA), located in St. Petersburg, Russia. A troll farm is a large group of interconnected computers working together to spread disinformation. The Russian employees posed as Americans. They developed fake news articles and commentary, which they released onto social media sites such as Facebook. They set up botnets consisting of millions of interconnected, automated

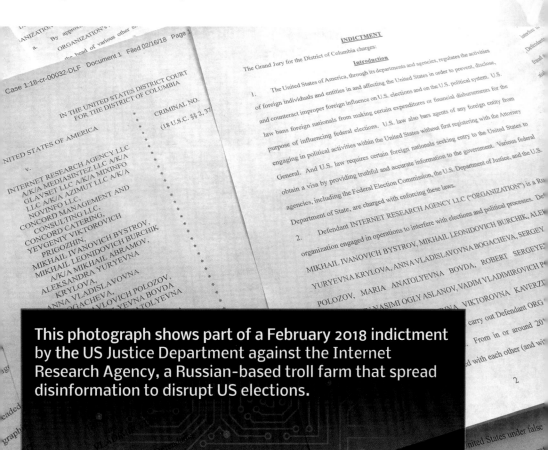

This photograph shows part of a February 2018 indictment by the US Justice Department against the Internet Research Agency, a Russian-based troll farm that spread disinformation to disrupt US elections.

computer programs, or bots, to spread the misinformation farther and faster.

In February 2018, the US Justice Department indicted thirteen Russians and three Russian entities, including the IRA, in these illegal attacks on the US election. In July, they indicted another twelve members of Russia's GRU, or foreign military intelligence unit. Because they are all located in Russia, these people and organizations will likely never be prosecuted. They remained active, targeting the 2018 midterm elections in similar ways.

The rise of online social media has unleashed a host of new ethical problems. Attacks on elections target a right that defines American democracy. They seem especially unethical when conducted by an outside country. But, because the world's computer infrastructure is huge, complex, and interconnected, finding practical solutions to these problems is not easy. It will require years of work by thousands of cybersecurity specialists, politicians, and members of the general public.

CHAPTER 5

Popping the Filter Bubble

Filter bubbles are part of almost every internet user's world. But should they be? Most experts agree that filter bubbles cause problems in communication and that "popping" or bursting their personal filter bubbles would be good for users. Jon Martindale, writing for Digital Trends, gives reasons why. Since their beginnings, social media platforms such as Facebook and Google+ have been curating the information users receive. This curation pleases advertisers and makes users' experiences more pleasant and efficient. Martindale sees two different but related problems caused by the resulting filter bubbles. First, seeing only information you agree with results in a confirmation bias that gets worse over time. Second, because of the differences in information received by users, many users cannot connect and find areas of agreement. Thus, they are often unable to communicate and develop solutions to serious social problems. This situation is most obvious in the great disconnect between people with conservative and liberal political views.

Martindale also points out that it is easier for fake news to gain a foothold when filter bubbles are strong. Often, purveyors of fake news build on confirmation biases that people already have. They produce untrue stories that have a kernel of truth matching a particular bias, or they simply spread rumors and conspiracy theories. Fake news spreads far faster than truth, according to Brian Resnick, writing for Vox. Resnick quoted a 2018 *Science* study showing that falsehoods on Twitter reached 1,500 people six times faster than truth. False political news travels fastest. After the Parkland, Florida, school

After a mass shooting at Marjory Stoneman Douglas High School in Florida in February 2018, its students protested, demanding sensible gun laws. They were attacked with a fake news story.

shooting in February 2018, a group of Parkland students began actively to support gun control. A fake news story accused these young activists of being actors, rather than shooting survivors. The story reached hundreds of thousands of followers before Twitter and other social media platforms could shut it down. Such fake news stories often begin on Twitter and spread when ordinary users share them with friends.

How to Pop a Filter Bubble

There are two general ways to fight against the narrowed worldview that results from online filter bubbles. One is for individual users to pop their own personal filter bubbles. They take steps themselves to widen their search parameters and increase the variety of information they receive. The other way is for social media platform providers to alter their search algorithms. Providers might make overall changes in their approach to searches. Alternatively, they might become more transparent, showing users how their algorithms work and giving users more control over their own search results.

Individuals can broaden their personal search results in several ways. Search engines track users' personal information so they can return easily to sites they already know. Therefore, users must trick the search engine into forgetting what they preferred in the past. They can tweak the search engine's privacy settings to disable search results based on personal characteristics, such as location, age, gender, and interests. On Facebook, they can turn off "Instant Personalization," which gives user information to other sites. Users should regularly delete cookies, the tracking devices each website places on the user's browser. They can also completely disable the Tracking Cookies feature in the browser. DuckDuckGo is an alternative browser that is private because it does not track user

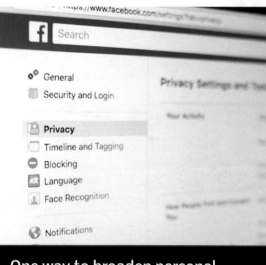

One way to broaden personal search results and break out of filter bubbles is to tweak the privacy settings on user apps, for example, changing the privacy settings on Facebook.

information. To become completely anonymous, users can download Torproject.org for free or Anonymizer.com for a fee. Users who are serious about receiving more balanced information can join social media groups of those whose opinions they disagree with. All these things help confuse the browser. Because the user is removing information that identifies his or her likely preferences, searches will return broader, more balanced results.

Martindale, in his Digital Trends article, suggests that algorithms could also change to limit the negative effects of filter bubbles. He refers to Eli Pariser, who, in his 2011 book, urged the gatekeepers of digital information—that is, programmers who write search algorithms—to encode aspects of journalistic integrity into their programming. Pariser believes that programmers could show civic responsibility by making algorithms more transparent. He thinks users should know the rules used and should have some control over the search. However, both Pariser and Martindale believe that the

Search engine analytics, such as the Google Analytics app, investigate and analyze search interactions. Analytics help in marketing and other functions and exemplify positive uses of internet filters.

best approach is for users to recognize their biases and pop their own filter bubbles. Research appears to support this idea. A Slate article by Stephanie Tam quotes a 2015 *Science* study by Facebook researchers showing that most polarization of political content results from user choices rather than algorithms.

Moral Bias and Search Results

Swedish journalist Andreas Ekström, in a 2015 TED Talk, points out that search results are always colored by our humanity and beliefs. Humans, deliberately or not, can control the contents of a search. Ekström illustrated his point with two examples of image searches in which humans intervened for ethical reasons.

When choosing photos, Google looks primarily at two things: the caption text and the file name. If both contain the words "Michelle Obama," all the results will likely be photos of Michelle Obama. But in 2009, a racist campaign distorted Obama's face to look like a monkey's face. They put Obama's name in both the caption and the file name. They uploaded the photo on Google, where it appeared in the search results. Google did not wait for their algorithms to self-correct automatically; their programmers removed the image manually.

Then, a 2011 terrorist attack in Norway killed seventy-seven people, mostly teenagers. Terrorist Anders Behring Breivik wanted publicity for his actions, said Ekström. But Swedish web developer Nikke Lindqvist decided to prevent Breivik from getting it. He urged his blog followers to upload photos of dog poop, with the terrorist's name in the caption and the image name. They did, and these photos appeared when his name was searched. This time, Google did not intervene. In both cases, for ethical reasons, humans intervened in the search results.

The Future of Filter Bubbles

Not everyone thinks filter bubbles are a bad thing. Shortly after Pariser's book was published, the MIT Media Lab released an editorial stating that, although Pariser was raising consciousness of the issue, he was also unnecessarily increasing fear. They pointed out the necessity of internet filters, starting with PageRank, Google's original filter. They gave examples of useful filters, such as spam filters, which eliminate unsolicited emails, and prediction engines, which help make predictions from data. Like others, MIT recommends improving filters by making them more transparent to the user.

Avoiding Bad New Bubbles

Angus Hervey, writing for Future Crunch, thinks the bad news bubble is more dangerous than the politically polarizing filter bubble. Writing in mid-2017, he gave a long list of bad news covered extensively in the press. This coverage included nuclear threats, chemical attacks, dictators, environmental disasters, bombings, shootings, and terrorist attacks around the world. Positive news is just as available but less well covered. How many people are aware, Hervey asked, of victories for LGBT and women's rights, improvements in world nutrition, and better income equality? How many know that fossil fuels are rapidly being replaced by clean, renewable energy? Or who knows about conservation wins for tigers, elephants, bees, forests, and oceans? According to Hervey, there is no incentive to report good news. But he argues that an objective view of the world requires balance, and balance requires optimism as well as pessimism.

For example, they think the search engine should give reasons for its recommendations. In addition, the filter should alter its behaviors based on a user's goals. For example, a person asking "How many pills per day do I take?" wants past behavior considered. A person researching the effects of lifestyle changes on health does not.

A 2016 study from the University of Twente, in the Netherlands, summarized the potential impacts of personalized media content and the resulting filter bubbles. Increased political polarization is leading to more extreme views and lower tolerance of others. This problem is more pronounced in the United States, with its two political parties, than in Europe, where most countries have many parties. Some also fear that filter bubbles will put democratic societies at risk, as people's news sources narrow and they develop knowledge gaps. However, the study authors caution that personalization algorithms are very new and the few studies done to

Some countries strive to combat political polarization by using social media apps. Here, an English-language version of WhatsApp presents tips for spotting fake news, just before an election in Pakistan.

date show only small effects. People are influenced by much more than their online activity. But the authors also caution that social media changes rapidly and must be continually monitored. They point out that panic does not help and that further studies will enable future policy decisions to be based on insight, rather than fear.

algorithm A process or set of rules used, especially by a computer, to solve a problem.

bias Prejudice in favor of, or against, a person, group, or thing, usually with an intent to be unfair; for example, racial bias.

botnets A network of bots, in which hundreds or thousands of automated computers infected with bots are interconnected and act together; can be used to spread viruses or misinformation.

bots Short for "robots"; automated computer programs that either run automatically or when they receive specific input; can be used for good (in search algorithms) or bad (to send disinformation in political campaigns).

cloud computing The process of storing and processing data on a network of remote servers rather than on local or personal servers; enables managing much larger amounts of information.

confirmation bias The tendency to interpret or search for information that confirms a person's preexisting beliefs or hypotheses.

conservative A person who dislikes change and accepts traditional values and attitudes in politics and social issues; also Republican or right wing.

cookies Small text files placed by each website on a person's browser; they enable the website to recognize users and keep track of their preferences.

curating Selecting, organizing, and presenting information to a target audience; for example, filter bubbles curate the information received by a user.

cyberbullying Using social media, texting, or email to post or share negative, harmful, or false content about another person, with the intent of humiliating or embarrassing that individual.

cybersecurity The field that specializes in designing protective hardware, software, and processes that thwart hackers and others seeking to bring down computer-controlled systems.

disinformation False and distorted information, often (but not always) spread over the internet.

echo chamber A situation in which a person hears only opinions and information with which he or she agrees; his or her existing biases are reinforced because he or she never hears contradictory ideas.

ethics The concepts involved in deciding questions of right and wrong; the system underlying responsible decision making by individuals, businesses, and society.

fake news A news story that can be demonstrated to be false but that is deliberately packaged to appear as true; it is meant to deceive the reader or listener.

filter bubble The intellectual isolation that results because social media users receive information that is selective and limited, rather than complete and unbiased.

gatekeeper The entity who determines what news or other information a person receives through media; for newspapers, this is a human editor, but for social media, it is digital (a computer program, or algorithm).

hacker A person who gains unauthorized access to data on a computer or computers.

IP address Internet Protocol address; a unique number assigned to each individual computer that identifies the computer, enabling it to communicate with other computers and to receive location-specific data, such as weather.

liberal A person with progressive views, who is open to new ideas and attitudes and is willing to discard or rethink traditional values; also Democratic or left wing.

open-minded filtering An approach in which a content filter occasionally lets random or unusual content pass through, so the user's experience is enriched by receiving broader information.

search engine A computer program designed to search for and identify information from an internet database, based on keywords; examples are Google, Safari, and Bing.

statisticians Experts in analyzing statistics, or large amounts of numerical data.

TED Talks Videos of experts giving public speeches on informational or educational topics.

troll farm A large, organized group of users working together to increase or generate online traffic with the purpose of sowing discord or spreading misinformation and disinformation.

Canadian's Internet Business

12158 82 Avenue
Surrey, BC V3W 5A6
Canada
Website: https://canadiansinternet.com
Facebook: @CanadianInternetBusiness
Twitter: @CanadianWebBiz
This organization works to empower Canadians with an interest in internet business and e-commerce. They provide resources, strategies, and information for Canadian audiences. They do not directly deal with filter bubbles, personalized searches, and the like.

Cyberbullying Research Center

Orlando, FL
Website: https://cyberbullying.org/teens-talk-works-stop
-cyberbullying
Facebook: @cyberbullyingresearch
Twitter: @onlinebullying
Instagram: @wordswound
This organization does research and provides information and assistance on cyberbullying. It provides resources for teens, parents, and educators. You can report instances of cyberbullying at cyberbullying.org/report.

Digital Analytics Association (DAA)

401 Edgewater Place, Suite 600
Wakefield, MA 01880 USA
(781) 876-8933
Website: https://www.digitalanalyticsassociation.org
Facebook: @digitalanalyticsassociation

Twitter: @DAAorg

The DAA studies data exclusively collected on websites. It seeks to understand and improve the digital world through professional development and community. Although based in the United States, it also sponsors conventions in Canada.

Facebook Newsroom

1 Hacker Way
Menlo Park, CA 94025
(650) 308-7300
Email: press@fb.com
Website: https://newsroom.fb.com/news
Facebook and Twitter: @facebook

Facebook's Newsroom site has up-to-date news about everything going on at Facebook, including changes in algorithms, internet security, and misinformation. The easiest way to find information is to type a keyword or phrase into the search window in the upper right.

Google Keyword

1600 Amphitheater Parkway
Mountain View, CA 94043
(650) 253-0000
Website: https://www.blog.google/outreach-initiatives
Facebook and Twitter: @Google

The Keyword is a Google blog that includes articles on topics related to Google and its business. Click the magnifying glass in the upper right to bring up a search window, and type in a key search word or phrase to find the information you want.

Pacer Center's Teens Against Bullying

8161 Normandale Boulevard
Minneapolis, MN 55437
(952) 838-9000
Website: https://www.pacerteensagainstbullying.org
Facebook: @PACERSNationalBullyingPreventionCenter
Twitter: @pacer_nbpc
This site is created by and for teens, to provide a place to address bullying, be heard, and act. It provides resources and information, including articles and videos.

School of Information

University of Michigan
4322 North Quad
105 South State Street
Ann Arbor, MI 48109-1285
(734) 764-9376
Website: https://www.si.umich.edu/research/center-social-media
-responsibility
Facebook: @uomsi
Twitter: @umsi
Instagram: @umschoolofinformation
This school, part of the University of Michigan, teaches people to create, use, and share knowledge to build a better world. They provide solutions and information to connect people, information, and technology.

Snapchat

63 Market Street
Venice, CA 90291
(310) 399-3339

Website: https://www.snapchat.com
Twitter: @Snapchat
The Snapchat website includes a Community page that provides a list of guidelines for safe use and a Safety Center that includes tips for staying safe and information for reporting inappropriate content.

Twitter

1355 Market Street, #900
San Francisco, CA 94103
(415) 222-9670
Website: https://about.twitter.com
Twitter: @Twitter
The Twitter website gives information about the company. In the About section is information on the company's values and on safety. In the Business section is information on targeting ads, analyzing tweets, and more. The Help section has information on safety and hacked accounts.

For Further Reading

Currie, Stephen. *Cyberbullying* (Thinking Critically). San Diego, CA: ReferencePoint Press, 2015.

Currie, Stephen. *Sharing Posts: The Spread of Fake News*. San Diego, CA: ReferencePoint Press, 2018.

Dakers, Diane. *Information Literacy and Fake News* (Why Does Media Literacy Matter?). New York, NY: Crabtree Publishing, 2018.

Greek, Joe. *Social Network-Powered Information Sharing* (A Teen's Guide to the Power of Social Networking). New York, NY: Rosen Publishing, 2014.

Gunderson, Josh. *Cyberbullying: Perpetrators, Bystanders & Victims*. N.p: CreateSpace Independent Publishing Platform, 2017.

Hand, Carol. *Everything You Need to Know About Fake News and Propaganda* (The Need to Know Library). New York, NY: Rosen Publishing, 2018.

Harris, Duchess, and Elisabeth Herschbach. *Your Personalized Internet*. Minneapolis, MN: ABDO Publishing, 2018.

Johanson, Paula, ed. *Online Filter Bubbles* (Opposing Viewpoints). New York, NY: Greenhaven Publishing, 2018.

Mara, Wil. *Fake News* (Global Citizens: Modern Media). Ann Arbor, MI: Cherry Lake Publishing, 2019.

Nakaya, Andrea C. *Is Social Media Good for Society?* (Issues in Society). San Diego, CA: ReferencePoint Press, 2017.

Parks, Peggy J. *Social Media* (Digital Issues). San Diego, CA: ReferencePoint Press, 2017.

Vance, Lucian. *Fake News and Media Bias* (Hot Topics). New York, NY: Lucent Press, 2018.

Bibliography

Anderson, Monica, and Jingjing Jiang. "Teens, Social Media & Technology 2018." Pew Research Center, Internet & Technology, May 31, 2018. http://www.pewinternet .org/2018/05/31/teens-social-media-technology-2018.

Baer, Drake. "The 'Filter Bubble' Explains Why Trump Won and You Didn't See It Coming." The Cut, November 9, 2016. https://www.thecut.com/2016/11/how-facebook-and-the -filter-bubble-pushed-trump-to-victory.html.

Bell, Karissa. "Apple News Wants to Fight Facebook-Induced Filter Bubbles." Mashable, June 25, 2018. https://mashable .com/2018/06/25/apple-news-midterm-elections /#c1LaLKv29OqK.

Bennett, Kate, and Betsy Klein. "Melania Trump Tackles 'Destructive and Harmful' Effects of Social Media." CNN, August 20, 2018. https://www.cnn.com/2018/08/20/politics /melania-trump-cyberbullying/index.html.

Borchers, Callum. "Facebook Invites You to Live in a Bubble Where You Are Always Right." *Washington Post*, January 14, 2018. https://www.washingtonpost.com/news/the-fix /wp/2018/01/14/facebook-invites-you-to-live-in-a-bubble -where-you-are-always-right/?utm_term=.6aa1904c617d.

Bozdag, Engin, and Job Timmermans. "Values in the Filter Bubbles, Ethics of Personalization Algorithms in Cloud Computing." Academia.edu. Retrieved August 4, 2018. http://www.academia.edu/1521454/Values_in_the_Filter _Bubble_Ethics_of_Personalization_Algorithms_in_Cloud _Computing.

Carnihan, Lee. "Pros and Cons of Personalized Search Results." LinkedIn, September 2, 2015. https://www.linkedin.com /pulse/warning-filtered-fight-back-lee-carnihan.

Curran, Dylan. "Are You Ready? Here Is All the Data Facebook and Google Have on You." *Guardian*, March 30, 2018. https://www.theguardian.com/commentisfree/2018/mar/28/all-the-data-facebook-google-has-on-you-privacy.

Davies, Dave. "How Google's Algorithms Work Now & Will Work in the Future." *Search Engine Journal*, June 7, 2017. https://www.searchenginejournal.com/google-algorithms-work-together/201226.

Delaney, Kevin J. "Filter Bubbles Are a Serious Problem with News, Says Bill Gates." Quartz Media, LLC, February 21, 2017. https://qz.com/913114/bill-gates-says-filter-bubbles-are-a-serious-problem-with-news.

Ekström, Andreas. "The Moral Bias Behind Your Search Results." TEDxOslo, January 2015. https://www.ted.com/talks/andreas_ekstrom_the_moral_bias_behind_your_search_results.

Elgersma, Christine. "17 Apps and Websites Kids Are Heading to After Facebook." Common Sense Media, July 17, 2017. https://www.commonsensemedia.org/blog/16-apps-and-websites-kids-are-heading-to-after-facebook.

Hervey, Angus. "Beware the Bad News Bubble." Future Crunch, April 19, 2017. https://medium.com/future-crunch/beware-the-bad-news-bubble-db3cdd964345.

Hills, Laura. "Answer These 12 Questions to Decide if Something Is Ethical?" Blue Pencil Sharpener, May 21, 2012. http://bluepencilinstitute.com/blog/2012/05/answer-these-12-questions-to-decide-if-something-is-ethical.

Lischka, Konrad, and Christian Stöcker. "Digital Public: Looking at What Algorithms Actually Do." The Conversation,

February 6, 2018. https://theconversation.com/digital-public -looking-at-what-algorithms-actually-do-91119.

Lum, Nick. "The Surprising Difference Between 'Filter Bubble' and 'Echo Chamber.'" Medium, January 27, 2017. https:// medium.com/@nicklum/the-surprising-difference-between -filter-bubble-and-echo-chamber-b909ef2542cc.

Martindale, John. "Forget Facebook and Google, Burst Your Own Filter Bubble." Digital Trends, December 6, 2016. https:// www.digitaltrends.com/social-media/fake-news-and-filter -bubbles.

McCammon, Sarah. "As the President Tweets Attacks, Melania Trump Speaks Out Against Cyberbullying." NPR, *All Things Considered,* August 20, 2018. https://www.npr.org/2018/08 /20/640234368/as-the-president-tweets-attacks-melania -trump-speaks-out-against-cyberbullying.

Morgan, Carleigh. "Why 'Popping' the Social Media Filter Bubble Misses the Point." Motherboard, November 16, 2016. https:// motherboard.vice.com/en_us/article/pgkxng/why-popping -the-social-media-filter-bubble-misses-the-point.

Oliveira, Aline. "Advantages and Disadvantages of Filtering Personalization Content." April 9, 2015. http://blogs.brighton .ac.uk/poa11/2015/04/09/advantages-and-disadvantages-of -filtering-personalization-content.

Pappas, Stephanie. "Social Media Cyber Bullying Linked to Teen Depression." *Scientific American,* June 23, 2015. https://www .scientificamerican.com/article/social-media-cyber-bullying -linked-to-teen-depression.

Pariser, Eli. "Beware Online 'Filter Bubbles.'" TED Talk, March 2011. https://www.ted.com/talks/eli_pariser_beware_online _filter_bubbles.

Pariser, Eli. *The Filter Bubble. How the New Personalized Web Is Changing What We Read and How We Think.* New York, NY: Penguin, 2011.

Poulsen, Kevin. "Exclusive: FBI Seizes Control of Russian Botnet." Daily Beast, May 23, 2018. https://www.thedailybeast.com /exclusive-fbi-seizes-control-of-russian-botnet.

Resnick, Brian. "False News Stories Travel Faster and Farther on Twitter than the Truth." Vox, March 19, 2018. https://www .vox.com/science-and-health/2018/3/8/17085928/fake-news -study-mit-science.

Resnick, Gideon. "How Pro-Trump Twitter Bots Spread Fake News." Daily Beast, November 17, 2016. https://www .thedailybeast.com/how-pro-trump-twitter-bots-spread-fake -news.

Roberts, Rachel. "Russia Hired 1,000 People to Create Anti-Clinton 'Fake News' in Key US States During Election, Trump-Russia Hearings Leader Reveals." *Independent*, March 30, 2017. https://www.independent.co.uk/news/world /americas/us-politics/russian-trolls-hilary-clinton-fake -news-election-democrat-mark-warner-intelligence -committee-a7657641.html.

Schwab, Pierre-Nicolas. "Big Data: 4 Types of Filter Bubbles." IntoTheMinds, November 14, 2016. https://www .intotheminds.com/blog/en/big-data-4-types-of-filter -bubbles.

Smith, Hannah. "The Ethical Issues of Personalization Online." Moz, June 26, 2011. https://moz.com/blog/the-ethical-issues -of-personalisation-online.

Sullivan, Danny. "Google's Personalized Results: The 'New Normal' that Deserves Extraordinary Attention." Search

Engine Land, December 7, 2009. https://searchengineland
.com/googles-personalized-results-the-new-normal-31290.

Summers, Timothy. "How the Russian Government Used
Disinformation and Cyber Warfare in 2016 Election—An
Ethical Hacker Explains." The Conversation, July 27, 2018.
https://theconversation.com/how-the-russian-government
-used-disinformation-and-cyber-warfare-in-2016-election
-an-ethical-hacker-explains-99989.

Thwaite, Alice. "What Is the Difference Between an Echo
Chamber and a Filter Bubble?" EchoChamber.club, December
26, 2017. https://echochamber.club/echo-chamber-filter
-bubble.

**Timberg, Craig. "Russian Propaganda Effort Helped Spread
'Fake News' During Election, Experts Say." *Washington Post*,
November 24, 2016.** https://www.washingtonpost.com
/business/economy/russian-propaganda-effort-helped
-spread-fake-news-during-election-experts-say.

University of Twente. "Gatekeeping." Communication Studies
Theories. Retrieved August 15, 2018. https://www.utwente
.nl/en/bms/communication-theories/sorted-by-cluster
/Media%2C%20Culture%20and%20Society/gatekeeping.

Weldon, Jeffrey. "The Filter Bubble: Disadvantages and
Advantages." IDST 325: University as a Design Problem,
Spring 2015. https://blogs.commons.georgetown.edu/idst
-325-spring2015/2015/02/02/the-filter-bubble-disadvantages
-and-advantages.

Index

About the Author

Carol Hand has a PhD in zoology with a specialization in ecology and environmental problems. She has taught at the college level, worked for standardized testing companies, developed multimedia science and technology curricula, and written many books for young people, mostly on science and technology. As a scientist, she understands the need for unbiased, factual information to make responsible decisions in all aspects of life.

Photo Credits

Cover Towqu Photography/Moment/Getty Images; pp. 4–5 NurPhoto/Getty Images; p. 7 Google screenshot. Google and the Google logo are registered trademarks of Google LLC, used with permission; p. 8 Bloomicon/Shutterstock.com; p. 11 Jon Shapley/Getty Images; p. 14 Leon Neal/Getty Images; p. 16 Smith Collection/Gado/Archive Photos/Getty Images; pp. 18, 32 Bloomberg/Getty Images; pp. 20–21 Monkey Business Images/ Shutterstock.com; pp. 22, 39 © AP Images; p. 25 Jeramey Lende/ Shutterstock.com; p. 27 Anatolii Babii/Alamy Stock Photo; p. 30 Jamie McCarthy/Getty Images; p. 35 ra2studio/Shutterstock .com; p. 36 © iStockphoto.com/dmbaker; p. 42 Pacific Press/ LightRocket/Getty Images; p. 43 Michael Candelori/Shutterstock .com; p. 44 BigTunaOnline/Shutterstock.com; p. 47 Aamir Qureshi/AFP/Getty Images; cover (top) and interior pages background image (circuit board) jijomathai/Shutterstock .com; additional interior pages circuit board image gandroni/ Shutterstock.com.

Design/Layout: Brian Garvey; Senior Editor: Kathy Kuhtz Campbell; Photo Researchers: Cindy Reiman and Nicole DiMella